THE LORD WAS WITH

JOSEPH

Learning to Live In the Presence of God...

SCOTT PAULEY

A resource from…

ENJOYING
THE
Journey

First Edition » Copyright © April, 2022 by Scott Pauley

All Scripture quotations are taken from the Authorized Version. Bible verses are in italics and references are footnoted for further study.

First published in 2022 by Enjoying the Journey in partnership with Faithworks Media. Enjoying the Journey exists to evangelize the lost with the gospel of Jesus Christ, encourage pastors and local churches, and equip believers to walk with God and serve Him each day. Through audio, video, and print resources we are seeking to preach the gospel, teach the Word of God, and reach this generation for Christ.

Faithworks Media provides high-quality church print resources and evangelistic material which *"adorn the doctrine of God our Saviour in all things."*

Cover design and layout by Stephen Troell
Editing, proofreading, and assistance by Tammy Jones, Lauren Pauley, and Monroe Roark. Special thanks to Kyle Austin, Micah Hendry, and Jesse Latta for early reading of the manuscript and their encouragement with the project.

ISBN 978-1-958301-00-5
eISBN 978-1-958301-01-2
Printed in the United States of America

FAITHWORKS ◊ MEDIA
"For the Furtherance of the Gospel" » **faithworks**media.com

To our precious children
Morgan, Lauren, and Grant
and to Isaac, our second son.

My prayer is that each of you will
learn the joy and blessing of living in the
presence of God every day.

*"I have no greater joy than to hear that
my children walk in truth."*

Contents

Foreword

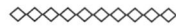

This book is not about Joseph. It is about the Lord who was with him, and who longs to be with you. There is only one main character in the history of the world. The rest of us are simply supporting characters in the divine drama. The Lord–Creator of all things, Savior of the world, and Judge of every man–is at work in the lives of normal people.

One of my favorite books to read is a good biography, but how much more when that biography is found in the Spirit-inspired words of Holy Scripture. God selected certain representative people to teach us by their example. Sometimes those examples are positive and sometimes they are negative. In Joseph's case, the Lord emphasizes his positive response to God in the midst of very negative circumstances.

D.L. Moody's life was changed forever when he heard a man named Henry Varley say, "The world has yet to see what God can do with a man fully consecrated to him." Moody said, "By God's help, I aim to be that man." Joseph was such a man: totally given to God and mightily used of God to make a difference in the world.

As you will see shortly, the open secret of Joseph's favor and fruitfulness was the presence of God in his life. *"The LORD was with Joseph."* In fact, all of Scripture is a reminder that God wants to be with man, and He wants man to be with Him.

When He created the world, He simply spoke it all into existence.[1] That is the power of the Word of God! One word from the Lord and everything is *"very good."* But when it came time to make man on the sixth day, He personally shaped man from the dust of the ground. The only thing recorded that God made with His own hands was man and woman. From the very beginning, His greatest desire was that our lives would be in His hands.

---

1 Genesis 1

This is why God came walking through the Garden of Eden. The Lord created man in his own image and for the intent of having fellowship with him.[2] On the sad day when man sinned in the garden, the voice of the Lord God made them afraid. Sin will do that. They ran and hid from the Holy One. I imagine that every day before they had run toward the voice and not away. Every person's life is moving in one direction or another.

One of the saddest expressions in Scripture is given regarding the day that Adam and Eve sinned in the Garden of Eden. The Bible says that they *"hid themselves from the presence of the LORD God."*[3] Our first parents were the beginning of a long line of people headed in the wrong direction. In the next chapter, we read that their son Cain did the same thing: *"And Cain went out from the presence of the LORD."*[4]

Sin always separates us from God. Our sin nature never seeks after Him. *"There is none that seeketh after God."*[5] Yet God continues to seek after man. From the start, man was the runner and God was the Seeker. Some things never change.

---

2 Genesis 1:26-28
3 Genesis 3:8
4 Genesis 4:16
5 Romans 3:11

And so, in every generation, God has sought individuals who would walk with Him. Enoch walked with God.[6] Noah walked with God.[7] Abraham was the friend of God.[8] God called Moses to come up and be with Him in the mount for forty days. He called the children of Israel to mount Sinai to speak with them. He established a Tabernacle, and later a Temple, where His presence would come down. God has always longed to be with His people.

Then Jesus came. God became a man without ceasing to be God. When Christ came to earth, Matthew 1:23 records, *"Behold, a virgin shall be with child, and shall bring forth a son, and they shall call his name Emmanuel, which being interpreted is, God with us."* The reason Christ came was so that the Lord could be with every single one of us. *"And the Word was made flesh, and dwelt among us."*[9]

Those first followers of Christ had the distinct privilege of spending three and a half years with Jesus. It was their first calling and their highest privilege. *"He ordained twelve that they should be with him…"*[10] What they would later become

---

6   Genesis 5:24
7   Genesis 6:9
8   James 2:23
9   John 1:14
10 Mark 3:14

and do was secondary to the simple, powerful truth that they were with Jesus.

But, what about us? After the death, burial, and resurrection of Christ for our sins, He ascended back to Heaven. Just as He promised, He sent His Holy Spirit to live within every one of His followers. Why? Let the Lord Jesus explain it in His own words: *"And I will pray the Father, and he shall give you another Comforter, that he may abide with you for ever; Even the Spirit of truth; whom the world cannot receive, because it seeth him not, neither knoweth him: but ye know him; for he dwelleth with you, and shall be in you."*[11] God always makes a way for sinners to be reconciled and brought near. His heart is to be with His people and for His people to be with Him.

As we walk each day in the Lord's presence, His character and nature begin to be developed in our lives. The greatest honor of any life is for others to see Christ in us, to observe that the Lord is with us.

Perhaps you do not know for certain that you belong to Jesus Christ and that He belongs to you. I have good news. The Lord said, *"All that the Father giveth me shall come to*

---

11 John 14:16-17

me; and him that cometh to me I will in no wise cast out."[12] The Heavenly Father sent His perfect Son to earth to die for the sins of every man. He loves you. If you will come to Him in repentance and faith, He will forgive your sin and come into your life. Christ will not turn you away. Will you come to Him?

If you have never repented of your sin and placed your faith in Christ as your personal Savior, you can do so right now. *"That if thou shalt confess with thy mouth the Lord Jesus, and shalt believe in thine heart that God hath raised him from the dead, thou shalt be saved. For with the heart man believeth unto righteousness; and with the mouth confession is made unto salvation."*[13] Call on Him now: *"God, be merciful unto me a sinner."*[14] He will hear your prayer and come to live with you forever. (For more on knowing Christ, read the Enjoying the Journey section in the back of this book.)

The greatest goal in life is God Himself. Soon we will see Him face to face. Jesus said: *"Let not your heart be troubled: ye believe in God, believe also in me. In my Father's house*

---

12 John 6:37
13 Romans 10:9-10
14 Luke 18:13

are many mansions: if it were not so, I would have told you. I go to prepare a place for you. And if I go and prepare a place for you, I will come again, and receive you unto myself; that where I am, there ye may be also." Shortly, those who belong to the Lord will be with Him forever!

You do not have to wait until you die or Christ returns to live in the presence of God! Let's study the life of Joseph together and discover the joy and power of living in the presence of the Lord today. The Lord has much to teach all of us through His Word. You will notice that each section begins with an action verb. This is because the aim of the following pages is not merely information; it is personal application. Read this book to know God better and to follow Him more closely.

Until that wonderful day that we are all together with the Lord, it is my prayer that you will learn to live consciously in God's presence.

Scott Pauley
Beckley, West Virginia
April 2022

"The LORD Was With Joseph"

The story of Joseph, found in the book of Genesis, is an example of what it means to give all that you have to God early in life, and then watch Him give back to you His best for the rest of your life.

Do you want God's best for your life? Of course you do. The problem is that while everyone wants the product, not everyone likes the process. We all want God to give us His best but we struggle to give Him our best. Joseph understood that, in order to find God's way, he would have to give himself entirely to the Lord. This is true in every generation. Thousands of years later, Paul wrote,

> *I beseech you therefore, brethren, by the mercies of God, that ye present your bodies a living sacrifice, holy, acceptable unto God, which is your reasonable service. And be not conformed to this world: but be ye transformed by the renewing of your mind, that ye may prove what is that good, and acceptable, and perfect, will of God.*[1]

There is a phrase found four times in Genesis 39 that is a good summary of the entire life of Joseph: *"the Lord was with Joseph."* This divine repetition reminds us of the necessity of God's blessing. We need God!

Verse 2: *"And the Lord was with Joseph ..."*

Verse 3: *"And his master saw that the Lord was with him..."*

Verse 21: *"But the Lord was with Joseph ..."*

Verse 23: *"... because the Lord was with him ..."*

---

1   Romans 12:1-2

2

THE LORD WAS WITH JOSEPH

What a beautiful progression is found in this passage. The initial statement in verse 2 reveals that God's presence in Joseph's life was the same in Egypt as it was in Canaan. God is not bound by geography or circumstances. In verse 3, we find that other people–even unbelievers–observed the presence of God in Joseph's life. You don't have to tell anyone when the Lord is with you; they will recognize it on their own. It was true when Moses came off the mountain.[2] It was evident in the disciples *"that they had been with Jesus."*[3]

The greatest thing anyone could say about your life is that the Lord was with you.

By the time we find Joseph in verse 21, he was facing great difficulty, and yet God was still with him. Having Him with you does not mean your life is going to always be smooth; it

---

2   Exodus 34:29
3   Acts 4:13

means He is going to bring you through whatever you have to deal with in life. The Lord is with you.

The final reference in verse 23 uses the word *"because"* and teaches us that every good thing that came into Joseph's life was due to the Lord's presence. God is always the first cause. So many people are trying to make life better, to be somebody, to go somewhere. In Joseph's experience, we are reminded that every good thing is brought to our lives by God. Nothing is too hard for God, but the difficulty often is getting out of God's way so He can bring His best to us.

The greatest thing anyone could say about your life is that the Lord was with you. It is the best epitaph by which one could be remembered. It is the distinguishing characteristic of the blessed life.

Do you want to be blessed by the Lord? Remember, His blessing is not measured in material things; it is manifested in His presence. When you get the Blesser, you get the blessings.

Many are searching for the right college, the best career path, the perfect spouse, or the next step in life.

These pursuits aren't necessarily wrong, they simply are not as important as pursuing God. Pursue God, and He will bring along with Him every good thing He has planned for your life.

[God's] blessing is not measured in material things; it is manifested in His presence.

In this portion of the Bible, the name that is used for God is written this way: "LORD." The significance of this name must not be missed. "LORD" was the personal and powerful name Yah-weh. It was reverenced by the Jews as God's covenant name–the name of the One who made promises and always keeps His Word. You have His good name on it!

This study is not about the faithfulness of Joseph but about the faithfulness of the Lord in his life. It is important to note that this expression is not reserved for Joseph alone.

THE LORD WAS WITH JOSEPH

Scripture tells us that the Lord was with the judges.[4] He was with Samuel.[5] He was with David.[6] He was with Ahaz.[7] He was with Phineas.[8] He was with John the Baptist.[9] Though there is a particular emphasis in the life of Joseph, the presence of the Lord is never reserved for one person!

In fact, when the Lord Himself comes to indwell every believer, we can confidently believe that the Lord is with every one of His children. The question is whether we will allow His holy presence to control every area of our lives.

These simple lessons are *from* the life of Joseph, but they are *about* the Lord. If you will apply them, they can be the guiding and guarding principles of your life as well.

---

4   Judges 2:18
5   1 Samuel 3:19
6   1 Samuel 18:12,14
7   2 Kings 18:7
8   1 Chronicles 9:20
9   Luke 1:66

Seeing the Lord
In Your Past

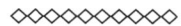

Everything is clearer in retrospect, or as many say: "Hindsight is 20/20." From where we stand, there is no doubt that the Lord was with Joseph. To get a proper perspective of how God was at work in his life, it is important to go back to the beginning of Joseph's story in Genesis 37. If you want to understand your present and your future, you, likewise, have to deal with your past.

Many people get fixated on their past without ever bringing into focus how the Lord was working in it. They are stuck on something that happened to them years ago, a bad decision they made, or someone who did them wrong. If you are ever going to become the man or woman God created you to become, at some point, you have to overcome your past and see that the Lord was at work in every detail and difficulty.

In case you haven't heard, I have some good news for you: God is not against you! He is actually for you, and as Paul wrote in Romans 8:31, *"If God be for us, who can be against us?"*

Notice how the story begins in Genesis 37:1-2: *"And Jacob dwelt in the land wherein his father was a stranger, in the land of Canaan. These are the generations of Jacob. Joseph, being seventeen years old, was feeding the flock with his brethren; and the lad was with the sons of Bilhah, and with the sons of Zilpah, his father's wives: and Joseph brought unto his father their evil report."*

Joseph's age was specifically given. He was on the threshold of being an adult, at a point in life where young people today face so many questions and possibilities about what the future might hold. They see so many decisions to be made. In fact, there are decisions to be made at every stage in life and it is vital that we consider God at every step along the way.

There are choices we will make, choices others will make that affect us, and choices God will make for us. You have complete control over your choices, a little control over others' choices, and no control over what God chooses. But His choice is always the right one.

There are decisions to be made at every stage in life and it is vital that we consider God at every step along the way.

Joseph appeared, by all accounts, to have a bright future. But that was all about to change as his brothers would soon sell him into slavery. It is important to remember that the beginning and ending of the story are not always the same, but God is always at work.

In this first introduction to Joseph, we are given an interesting picture: *"These are the generations of Jacob.*

Joseph, being seventeen years old, was feeding the flock with his brethren; and the lad was with the sons of Bilhah, and with the sons of Zilpah, his father's wives: and Joseph brought unto his father their evil report." He was a young man, in a good family, with a consistent job…and dealing with an *"evil report."* From the very beginning, there is evidence that there was much good in his life, and yet in the middle of that good, there was also evil. There are no perfect people and there is no perfect life.

On the surface, it may seem that Joseph had no trouble. Verse 3 says: *"Now Israel loved Joseph more than all his children, because he was the son of his old age: and he made him a coat of many colours."*

Occasionally, you may encounter someone who is considered the favorite child in a family. Others who are not treated this way can become bitter about it. There is no doubt that Joseph was Jacob's favorite and everyone knew it. All favor ultimately comes from God, and we all should realize that He grants or withholds favor because it fits in His divine purpose.[1]

Favor in one life too often becomes jealousy in others. In verses 4-5 we read: *"And when his brethren saw that their father loved him more than all his brethren, they hated him, and could not speak peaceably unto him. And Joseph dreamed a dream, and he told it his brethren: and they hated him yet the more."*

His tenure as prime minister of Egypt was still far off in the future, and he almost certainly could not even imagine such a life at this point. Years later, thousands of Egyptians watched him ride in a chariot through the streets and thought, "That is the life I want." But they were totally unaware of what he went through to get there.

We all live in a world structured by time. Nearly every person you know is on some kind of schedule. But it is interesting to note that God, who created time, is not at all governed by time. Instead, time lives in Him. Deuteronomy 33:27 declares that He is *"the eternal God."* That is how He knows *"the end from the beginning"* according to Isaiah 46:10.

---

1   Psalm 75:6-7

Psalm 90:2 says, *"Before the mountains were brought forth, or ever thou hadst formed the earth and the world, even from everlasting to everlasting, thou art God."* The expression *"everlasting to everlasting"* literally means "from vanishing point to vanishing point." Go all the way back to before Adam or the world itself existed. God was there. Go forward to where the world has burned up and everyone who lived here is gone. God will be there. He has always been and He always will be. And, yes, He is with us now!

The Lord has a much better view of life than we do and so His timetable is totally different from ours. You might think He is late, but He is not. You are just early. Like it or not, you are living on His schedule. Ecclesiastes 3:11 reminds us that he *"hath made everything beautiful in his time."*

This truth is important because what you believe about God determines what you believe about everything else. If you do not have the right perspective of God, you will never have the right perspective on the life He has given you.

If God is everlasting and lives in the eternal now, that means He is at work simultaneously in your past, your present, and your future. When you have your head down, stuck in the details of this particular day and what is being thrown at you in the present season of life, remember that God has a much better perspective than you do.

Things may seem unclear from your vantage point, but all is clear from Heaven. He has a much better view. We must get our eyes off of ourselves, our circumstances, and the people around us. Look to the Lord and know that He has always had His eyes on you.

See the Lord in *where* you were born.

Genesis 37:1 refers to Jacob and his family living *"in the land wherein his father was a stranger."* Joseph's grandfather Abraham had come from a faraway place, but by this time the family was right at home and well-established in the region.

Do you think it was a coincidence that Joseph was born to a family of promise in a land of promise? Of course not. God does nothing by accident.

Sometimes we reduce our lives to geography. "If I could just move there, I would be happy." No, you wouldn't. You would be just as miserable. You do not need a change of scenery; you need a change of heart. God does not work in the faraway land. He works right where you are.

He allowed Joseph to be born at that particular time and place in His divine providence. Today, He not only knows where you are, but He has you there at this moment for a reason. The Lord loves to work in ordinary places. God's greatest work might be in your hometown, in familiar surroundings. It could be in the very place you have been trying to escape so you can "make something of yourself." God wants to make something of you, and He begins right where you live. People are remembered for the extraordinary days in their lives, but they are made on their ordinary days.

Wherever you are at this moment, realize that it is not only the place of God's providence, but it is also just a temporary place. All of us are "just passing through." Joseph was born in Canaan, which we consider a happy and prosperous place. But the Lord only allowed him to live there 17 years before uprooting him and planting him somewhere else. It was in

Canaan where God prepared him for his time in Egypt and everything that he was supposed to do with his life.

If God wants to move you, let Him do it. His moves are always the right ones. We cannot see the finish line but He can. He is *"the author and finisher of our faith"* according to Hebrews 12:2. He is working right now to prepare you for what is to come.

See the Lord in *when* you were born.

I hear so many people complain about how bad things are today. They say, "This is a horrible time to live. It is very difficult to grow up in this generation." It should not be that way for the child of God. We have much to look forward to! As the songwriter noted, "This world is not my home; I'm just passing through." And while we are passing through, God in His providence has a plan for our lives.

Perhaps you've heard someone say that he wishes he had lived in a different time and things would have been so much better. The "good old days" are not what everyone has talked them up to be. Every generation has its troubles.

A group of college students was surveyed regarding what time in history they would prefer to live. The top three answers were the Victorian era of England, the "Roaring '20s" in the United States, and the Old West. Those all sound enjoyable for about a week, but as I read that report, I wondered what these people were thinking!

For the Christian, there can be no greater time in which to live than now. My grandparents' era is frequently referred to as the "greatest generation" because of the character, integrity, and sacrifice that was displayed back then. I understand that; we could use a dose of it today. But the greatest time to be alive is in the generation just before Jesus comes again.

No generation has had more opportunity and more obligation than the current one. I think it is a privilege that God would let us live near the end of the story. We have been called to live on the edge of eternity!

We know from verses 2-3 that Joseph was still a teenager while his father was an old man. He probably thought at times that the timetable was a bit messed up for him with an elderly parent and much older siblings who did not appreciate him. But God's chronology is always right.

The Bible says of the coming of Christ in Galatians 4:4-5, *"But when the fulness of the time was come, God sent forth his Son, made of a woman, made under the law, To redeem them that were under the law, that we might receive the adoption of sons."* The same God who had a perfect time for His Son has a perfect time for each of His children.

David said it well: *"But I trusted in thee, O Lord: I said, Thou art my God. My times are in thy hand…"*[2] He is always right on time. You can trust that God's timing in your life is perfect.

See the Lord in *who* He has brought into your life.

God used a variety of people to touch Joseph's life. He will do the same for you. In Jacob, Joseph had someone who loved him. Each of us has someone who has loved us and

---

2 Psalm 31:14-15

influenced us in a positive way. Praise God for every Jacob the Lord brings into your life. It could be a biological parent or perhaps a spiritual father or mother. God puts people in your life who love you to help you discover your divine purpose.

On the other hand, Joseph's brothers did not conceal their hatred of him. This was not just a standard sibling rivalry, but a family full of fleshly envy. Things tend to produce after their own kind, and a scheming, conniving Jacob produced several boys who were always trying to get ahead of each other. That is not God's way.

Most of us would see right away how Jacob would be the source of good for his young son. But it is interesting to note that it was not Joseph's loving father who got him to the eventual place of blessing, but his hateful brothers. This is an illustration of the principle stated in Psalm 76:10, *"Surely the wrath of man shall praise thee: the remainder of wrath shalt thou restrain."* An all-wise, all-powerful, all-loving God can use the worst of situations to bring His best into our lives. *"And we know that all things work together for good to them that love God, to them who are the called according to his purpose."*[3] He rules and He overrules.

Dr. Frank Sells, one of my favorite Bible teachers, used to tell us often, "Thank the Lord for everything the Lord uses to humble you." We can get so puffed up with our plans. There is nothing evil said in Scripture about Joseph, but in Genesis 37, you can see how a favored young man could become proud because of the things God was showing him.

> *Joseph's pit was actually the pathway to all that God had prepared for him.*

God has a way of letting the air out of your balloons, but that is actually His gift to you because everything that brings you low lifts you up. Whatever brings you to the end of yourself brings you nearer to Him.[4] It is powerful to think that the very people Joseph considered his enemies

---

3 Romans 8:28
4 Psalm 138:6

as a young man were the very ones who got him closer to where God wanted him to be.

Remember, when Joseph was thrown into a pit, it was actually the pathway to all that God had prepared for him. Your trial is not a dead end; it is a doorway to God's purpose in your life. When you are in the pits, look up! God has the future already planned.

Stop grumbling and complaining about whatever might have happened, and see the Lord in the twists and turns of life. Perhaps there is something now that you cannot figure out and you certainly cannot fix it. Even in the things you would never choose for yourself, remember that the Lord is with you.

God was not working to get Joseph to Egypt. That was the easy part. God wanted to bring Joseph nearer to Himself. The sooner you realize that this is the goal and you see Him working lovingly and patiently in your life, the more content you will be.

I find it interesting that this passage displays people who would help Joseph and then later be helped by him. We can be so selfish at times, even when we look to God for help. "Lord, I want you to show *me* something and do something for *me*." Has it dawned on you that the way God is working in your life right now is not just about you?

Joseph lived at a very difficult time in his family's history and God touched his life in such a way that he impacted an entire nation and generations to come for the glory of God. Thousands of years later, we are talking about the nation of Israel and all of the good that came through it because of one young man who began to see God at work even in the difficult circumstances of his life. When your life is in God's hands, you are a part of something much bigger than yourself.

See the Lord in *what* He has done in your life.

We are told in verse 5 that Joseph had a dream. God was stirring something within him. If something is just your idea, it will come and go. When God works it in you, it grows and grows. *"For the gifts and calling of God are without repentance."*[5]

Joseph's earthly father gave him a coat. His Heavenly Father gave him purpose. There are things which are so much more valuable than material gain, and one of them is the realization of why you are alive and what God would have you do. No one on earth can put that in you but the Lord. *"For it is God which worketh in you both to will and to do of his good pleasure."*[6]

God was not only working *in* him, He was working *for* him. His brothers were ready to put him out of their misery permanently, but there is a ray of hope in verse 21. *"And Reuben heard it, and he delivered him out of their hands; and said, Let us not kill him."*

It sounds like an incidental remark, but it was important to Joseph! Do you think Reuben came up with that plan all by himself? No. The Lord put in his heart the thought to spare his brother's life. God preserves and protects

---

5   Romans 11:29
6   Philippians 2:13

His servants. George Whitfield, the great preacher of the Great Awakening, once said, "I am immortal, until God is through with me."

Take a moment and consider all of the things God has kept from you, most of which you do not even know. If you are alive right now, it is because God has let you live and He has done so for a reason. Everything He has put into your life is so that He can bring something wonderful out of your life.

To live a God-conscious life, you must begin by seeing the Lord in your past.

More evidence of God at work is found in verse 28 when the Midianites came along at just the right time. The verse concludes, *"and they brought Joseph into Egypt."* That was the place where he needed to be so he could do the greatest work of his life for God, and God did a great work to get him there.

Do you believe that God is able to take you from where you are at this moment to the place He has planned for you? The Bible says in Philippians 1:6, *"Being confident of this very thing, that he which hath begun a good work in you will perform it until the day of Jesus Christ."*

God does not need your help to adjust His plans. He has been with you from the very beginning and wants *"to give you an expected end."*[7] If you are going to live a God-conscious life, you must begin by seeing the Lord in your past.

Stop letting a single blot on your story affect you, and remember that the Lord is greater than all of your failures. Likewise, don't get stuck in a past blessing and miss out on the blessings He has for you today. You cannot live in the burdens or the blessings of yesterday.

For Joseph in Genesis 37, the future was uncertain. The circumstances were unexpected. The people were unpredictable. None of that by itself sounds very promising, but there was one other detail to consider: *"The LORD was with him."*

---

7   Jeremiah 29:11

24

Action Page

One truth...

Learn from your past but do not live in it.

Memorize and Meditate...

"And we know that all things work together for good to them that love God, to them who are the called according to his purpose." Romans 8:28

Ask and Answer...

1. *What is something unique in Joseph's past that the Lord turned for good later in his life?*

2. *What attribute of God stands out to you from this portion of Joseph's life?*

Next Steps on My Journey...

Write a short story of how God has protected and guided to this point in your life. Do not major on minors or emphasize negatives. Think about how the Lord has been with you and speak most about Him. Share an appropriate testimony on social media, in conversation with someone, or with a group of fellow believers this week.

Remembering the Lord in Your Temptations

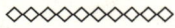

Joseph's example has been the centerpiece of sermons from the earliest days of the church. For instance, in Acts 7, we have a recorded message from Stephen that mentions him. Listen to the preacher's words, *"And the patriarchs, moved with envy, sold Joseph into Egypt: but God was with him."*[1] Does that sound vaguely familiar? The New Testament reminds us of the most important thing about this Old Testament character. It was not his appearance

---

1   Acts 7:9

or his accomplishments. It was not his circumstances or his connections. The one thing that set Joseph apart from others was the presence of the Lord.

Joseph's extended family, the children of Israel, would understand the importance of this in the generations that followed. When Moses was called on to lead the nation, he asked God for one thing: he wanted the presence of God to go with them. *"For wherein shall it be known here that I and thy people have found grace in thy sight? is it not in that thou goest with us? so shall we be separated, I and thy people, from all the people that are upon the face of the earth."*[2] It is the presence of God that separates us! When the Lord is with you, you have all that you need.

We like to think that at some point we would get past all of the stress, struggle, and strain of life and have smooth sailing all the way to Heaven. That day never comes. We are sinners, surrounded by other sinners, and we live in a sin-cursed world. In fact, the greatest struggle I have is not with anyone else–it is with me!

---

2 Exodus 33:16

THE LORD WAS WITH JOSEPH

Every morning, I look in the mirror at my biggest enemy. I drag him around everywhere I go. It is my fallen nature, the old man, the flesh that gives me the most trouble. You can dress it up, give it a Bible, and let it do religious things, but it is still just sinful flesh. We all battle the flesh. How do we gain victory? We must remember that, in the middle of our temptations, the Lord is with us. That is the secret.

In the early days, Joseph had a difficult time with people. The trials in Genesis 37 were based on his circumstances and others around him. Perhaps he thought to himself, "If I can just get through this trial, I'll be fine."

He eventually found himself in Egypt, which in Scripture is frequently a picture of this world system. In Joseph's day, that country was a place of tremendous idolatry and immorality. I have had the opportunity to visit the land of Egypt and it was one of the most spiritually oppressive places I have ever been. I believe that is partly because of the curse of God on that land and the residual effects of it. Sin always brings lasting consequences.

THE LORD WAS WITH JOSEPH

By the time we see Joseph in Genesis 39, he is not only dealing with others, but with himself. Nothing evil is recorded of Joseph but that doesn't mean that he did not have a sin nature or selfish desires. It simply means that he made the right choice and did not allow himself to excuse sin or blame others. It is easy to blame someone else for our failures, but each of us make our own choices. We are about to see that Joseph has a great decision to make.

It is interesting to note that the previous chapter, Genesis 38, does not mention Joseph at all. Instead it tells a story about Judah, one of his brothers. Judah made a tragic choice to follow after the flesh and yield to temptation. But in Genesis 39, Joseph made the choice to follow after the Lord and keep himself clean and pure. This stark contrast serves as a reminder that each of us have our temptations, each of us have choices to make, and each of us are personally accountable to God.

Every day you must choose whether you are going to be Judah or Joseph. And you will be one or the other. There is no way to avoid it. Just remember that choices have consequences. "*And the world passeth away, and the lust thereof: but he that doeth the will of God abideth for ever.*"[3]

Notice how this chapter of Joseph's life begins:

> *And Joseph was brought down to Egypt; and Potiphar, an officer of Pharaoh, captain of the guard, an Egyptian, bought him of the hands of the Ishmeelites, which had brought him down thither. And the* Lord *was with Joseph, and he was a prosperous man; and he was in the house of his master the Egyptian. And his master saw that the* Lord *was with him, and that the* Lord *made all that he did to prosper in his hand. And Joseph found grace in his sight, and he served him: and he made him overseer over his house, and all that he had he put into his hand. And it came to pass from the time that he had made him overseer in his house, and over all that he had, that the* Lord *blessed the Egyptian's house for Joseph's sake; and the blessing of the* Lord

---

was upon all that he had in the house, and in the field. And he left all that he had in Joseph's hand; and he knew not ought he had, save the bread which he did eat. And Joseph was a goodly person, and well favoured.[4]

So far, so good! Wouldn't it be nice if the story stopped at the end of verse 6? Unfortunately, it did not. The temptation comes in verses 7-9:

And it came to pass after these things, that his master's wife cast her eyes upon Joseph; and she said, Lie with me. But he refused, and said unto his master's wife, Behold, my master wotteth not what is with me in the house, and he hath committed all that he hath to my hand; There is none greater in this house than I; neither hath he kept back any thing from me but thee, because thou art his wife: how then can I do this great wickedness, and sin against God?

---

4   Genesis 39:1-6

Here we see one of the great tests Joseph faced, one that we all face. It is a pass/fail test. It is the test of our integrity.

It is one thing to say that the Lord is with us. It is quite another to practice the presence of God and to acknowledge His holiness in the presence of our own temptations.

We read more than one reference in this passage about the prosperity of Joseph, and there is no doubt that many who saw him thought he was just one of those people who everything he touched turned to gold. But that impression came from only seeing the peripheral, not what was in his heart. As 1 Samuel 16:7 tells us, *"Man looketh on the outward appearance, but the LORD looketh on the heart."*

The world will judge you by your prosperity; God will judge you by whether you live in His presence.

The secret to Joseph's life was internal, not external. It had little to do with how he was in public or what everyone else saw, and everything to do with his private life and what God knew about him.

None of us are what we perceive ourselves to be or what we try to show others. We are what God knows us to be.

THE LORD WAS WITH JOSEPH

In a social media world, with all of its filters, a person can portray a certain aura. But God knows you and all of the deep, secret things of your life. He knows every thought, desire, motive, and choice made in the secret place.[5]

There was someone else in the house with Joseph and the wife of Potiphar — the Lord was in that house.

If you are a child of God, He is with you everywhere you go. It is only when you remember His presence that you are empowered by Him to get victory in your life over the temptation that inevitably will come.

Some people think it is strange that temptation comes after salvation, but it is not strange at all. The Bible says in 1 Corinthians 10:13, *"There hath no temptation taken you but such as is common to man: but God is faithful, who will not suffer you to be tempted above that ye are able; but will with the temptation also make a way to escape, that ye may be able to bear it."* The escape is the presence of God.

I remember watching a man who was training dogs. It was fascinating to watch those animals sit perfectly still with a

---

5   Jeremiah 17:10; Ecclesiastes 12:14

treat held right in front of their faces! They would not move until given the command. What was the secret? They had been trained to look past the treat that was immediately in front of them and to keep their eyes fixed on their master.

The only way to break an attraction, an addiction, an affection is to find a greater desire. As the Lord becomes our great pursuit, He will begin to change us. You cannot remove temptation but you can look beyond the temptation to the God who is greater. Keep your eyes on the Master and He will give you restraint and power you do not have on your own.

The only way to break an
attraction, an addiction, an affection
is to find a greater desire.

If a man like Joseph had to deal with temptation, you can be sure that you and I will. We all have sinful tendencies. In fact, we all have besetting sins. God calls it *"the sin which doth so easily beset us.*[6] You know the one. Your besetting sin is the one that keeps getting you off track and that you are confessing constantly, saying, "I'll never do that again." Then you find yourself right back there. It is what you run to when you are weak, weary, and discouraged–when you should be running to Jesus.

Once you identify it, how do you get victory over it? In recent days, I believe the Lord has started to show me one of the besetting sins of my life. It may not sound all that bad to some, but it is a horrible sin.

This besetting sin is forgetfulness. It is forgetting how good God is and how awful sin is. How quickly I forget the brokenness that brought me back to the Lord and the holy vows I made to Him. When you forget those things, it is easy to get back into sin. It is easy to follow after the wickedness of this world when you forget the goodness of God. It is easy to make excuses and exceptions in your life when you forget that you have been consecrated to Him.

---

6   Hebrews 12:1

Part of the reason Joseph was kept so pure and clean was because he was someone who did not forget. The only training he had was what he received in the first seventeen years of his life. His captors were not serving the true God in Egypt. Everything he knew about God had been instilled in him as a young person, but it got in him so deeply that when his father and his brothers were not around to look over his shoulder, and everything familiar was hundreds of miles away, he recognized that the Lord God Almighty was still with him.

The difficult thing to do in the Christian life is not to make a spiritual decision, but to keep it. Getting right with God is easy; staying right with God is something that must be worked at every day. How do we stay clean? Stay close to the Lord. We must remember the Lord in our temptations.

Keep these spiritual truths from Joseph's example in your spiritual memory.

Remember that the tests often come after blessing.

In verses 2-6, Joseph had enjoyed great prosperity, but tests often come after great blessing. Verse 7 begins, *"And it came to pass after these things…"* Everything was going so well, when suddenly he was faced with the biggest temptation of his life. *"Wherefore let him that thinketh he standeth take heed lest he fall."*[7] It is after the biggest victories that we can fight the biggest spiritual battles.

When you think to yourself, "I've got this whipped," you had better be very careful. If you have the devil on the run on one side, remember that he will strategically come around from the other side. The Bible says in 1 Peter 5:8, *"Be sober, be vigilant; because your adversary the devil, as a roaring lion, walketh about, seeking whom he may devour."*

It is shocking to me how quickly I can go from spiritual to fleshly. I can sense the presence of God, worship Him, pray sincerely to Him, only to walk out the door and forget

---

7   1 Corinthians 10:12

what the Lord has done in my heart. The life of purity and blessing must be a moment by moment walk in the presence of a holy God.

Remember that when no one else is watching, God is.

In verse 9, Joseph emphasized what yielding to this temptation would potentially do to him, and reminded the woman that she was not his wife but someone else's. She embodied what Proverbs 2:16 dubbed the *"strange woman"* and Jude 7 called *"strange flesh."* What does the Bible mean when it calls someone or something *"strange"*?

We usually associate such an expression with appearances, but looks often has nothing do with it. Many years ago, I was walking with our little girl though a shopping mall. We passed a man whose whole appearance was a little frightening and marked by certain evil things. As we passed, to my utter dismay, she said loudly, "What is wrong with that guy?" I wanted to keep moving as quickly as possible and say something clever later, but the Holy Spirit urged me to tell her that very likely he did not know the Lord and was searching for something. Sin can look strange, but it often looks very normal, even beautiful.

The true definition of *"strange"* in these passages is that it does not belong to us; it is different than what God intended. The old saying "the grass is always greener on the other side" has a spiritual connotation to it, because there is something in our sin nature that tells us we are missing out on something. We may have many good things, but there is something we don't have, so we convince ourselves that we need it.

Think for a few moments about how good God has been to you–the opportunities you have had, the truth you have heard from having access to His Word, the people He has put in your life. His blessings should lead all of us to repentance.[8] Intentionally thinking on the goodness of God will keep your heart from evil.

When fighting off the advances of Potiphar's wife, Joseph mentioned the master of the house who had entrusted him

---

8   Romans 2:4

with so much. It was true that his master was not around, but Joseph immediately acknowledged the Master who was always there. For all that Potiphar had given to him, he recognized that God had given him so much more.

Remember that all sin is against God.

Joseph knew, "That woman is not mine. She belongs to another man." It was important that Joseph recognized who his master was and whose wife the woman was. Ultimately, it was most important that he remembered who he belonged to and who God *is*. Verse 9 ends, "*… how can I do this great wickedness, and sin against God?*" Regardless of how far he advanced in Egypt, Joseph knew he was not God. And no matter how secret the sin, there was no way to hide it from God.

Joseph did not mention sinning against Potiphar (although adultery with his wife would have been so) or sinning against his own body (although adultery is exactly that according to 1 Corinthians 6:18), but he stated that this sin would ultimately be against God. Sin affects many people, but it is always, first, and most terribly, a sin against God.

According to Proverbs 15:3, *"The eyes of the LORD are in every place, beholding the evil and the good."* Do you remember the story of Achan in Joshua 7? He thought no one saw him take the spoils from Jericho, but God saw him, and the result was tragedy for the Israelites, as well as his own family. God sees everything. There is a certain consciousness of God that is necessary if you are going to live the Christian life.

If we started seeing sin like God sees it, we would hate it. The reason you love your sin is because you see it like you see it. We love this world because we see it through the eyes of flesh instead of from Heaven's vantage point. But if you could see your sin and what it did to Jesus on the cross, you would hate it. If you saw the damnation it will bring to souls, the destruction it will bring to families, and the corruption it would bring to other people's lives, you would hate it.

Joseph was spiritual enough even as a young man to see that all sin was against God–His holiness, His love and His law. When we sin, we take a position of opposition to God.[9] That is a very dangerous place to be. I know because I have been there.

Every believer eventually recognizes that his or her sin is against God; it is just a matter of when that recognition takes place. Consider the very different experiences of Joseph and David.

King David's initial interaction with Bathsheba led to adultery and eventually to murder. It was offensive to many people, certainly to Bathsheba's husband Uriah whose life was cut short by the coverup. However, in the middle of his great confession in Psalm 51, he makes this statement to the Lord in verse 4: *"Against thee, thee only, have I sinned, and done this evil in thy sight: that thou mightiest be justified when thou speakest, and be clear when thou judgest."*

Both of these men recognized that their sin was against God, but Joseph recognized it *before* he sinned and

---

9   Romans 8:7; James 4:4

David did so *afterward*. If you wait until after the sin to acknowledge God's presence, you have waited too late. Indeed, there are some things we simply would not do if we were conscious that we were in the holy presence of God.

Remember that temptation will never go away.

We are told in verse 10, *"And it came to pass, as she spake to Joseph day by day, that he hearkened not unto her, to lie by her, or to be with her."* We do not live the Christian life one day a week, or a few days a month. It is every single day, year after year, *"day by day."*

Several years ago on our Enjoying the Journey broadcast, we did a study of the daily Christian life and examined each use of the word *"daily"* throughout the Bible. We learned that there are many daily things we are commanded to do. But we all must adjust to the fact that every day is a temptation day.

Today is temptation day and so is tomorrow. Even the Lord's day is temptation day. The devil never stops. Consider what happened at the end of 40 days of tempting Jesus, as detailed in Luke 4:13. *"And when the devil had ended all the temptation, he departed from him for a season."* That means he eventually came back. Even his temptation of Christ was not confined to a single episode. Satan will always return.

The disciples asked Jesus in Luke 11:1, *"Lord, teach us to pray."* That led to Christ giving His followers what we commonly refer to as "The Model Prayer." It is interesting to note the progression in verses 3-4: *"Give us day by day our daily bread. And forgive us our sins; for we also forgive every one that is indebted to us. And lead us not into temptation; but deliver us from evil."* There is a connection between receiving the spiritual nourishment we need every day so we can resist the temptation and evil all around us. Every day we need God's strength because every day we fight the enemy.

Do you see the divine order? Avoiding *"temptation"* helps to keep us from *"evil."* One vital key to avoiding sin is avoiding temptation! People frequently speak of "falling" into sin as if it were an accident, when we are usually walking so close to its edge that we can do little else but land in it eventually. Deal with sin at its root and you will avoid *"the great transgression."*[10]

Remember that if you want to avoid sin you must get as far away from it as possible.

Here is some wise advice: *"Avoid it, pass not by it, turn from it, and pass away."*[11] God's Word tells us that Joseph did not even want to have a conversation with Potiphar's wife. He was getting as far away from trouble as possible. Contrast that with what Samson did with Delilah: *"He told her all his heart."*[12] Samson's story ended in tragedy, while Joseph's story ended in triumph.

You may think, "I'm not going to get serious with that person, but they are just easy to talk to." That is how it works. If you talk long enough and share enough, you will give your heart away and find yourself perhaps in love with

---

10 Psalm 19:12-13
11 Proverbs 4:15
12 Judges 16:17

the wrong person. Your heart, not your body, is the most precious thing you can give someone.

Stop making it easy on yourself to sin.

Joseph knew he should not listen to Potiphar's wife or even be in the house when she was around. As Paul wrote in Romans 13:14, *"But put ye on the Lord Jesus Christ, and make not provision for the flesh, to fulfill the lusts thereof."* Stop making it easy on yourself to sin.

We are commanded in Hebrews 12:1 to *"lay aside every weight, and the sin"* because weights are very often the things that lead to the sin. They are things that, in and of themselves might not be all bad, but they are keeping us from living in victory. Stop seeing how close you can get to sin before blowing it, and decide instead to get as far away from it as possible. *"Abstain from all appearance of evil."*[13]

---

13 1 Thessalonians 5:22

Remember there is a time to run.

Even as we work to avoid temptation, you can be sure that somehow, some way, someday it will come. Verses 11-12 say, *"And it came to pass about this time, that Joseph went into the house to do his business; and there was none of the men of the house there within. And she caught him by his garment, saying, Lie with me: and he left his garment in her hand, and fled, and got him out."* This was a grown man running for his life. He may have been the boss of the house, but he knew to flee because he did not trust himself.

For each of us, there will also be a time to run. When that time comes, run to Jesus. Run to the Lord and from yourself and the world. Paul noted several examples of when it is time to run.

"Flee fornication."[14]

"But thou, O man of God, flee these things."[15]

"Flee also youthful lusts."[16]

---

14 I Corinthians 6:18
15 I Timothy 6:11
16 II Timothy 2:22

Temptation itself is not sin but your response to that temptation may be. Remember that our sinless Lord, *"was in all points tempted like as we are, yet without sin."*[17] You can endure temptation and stay pure! Martin Luther said, "You cannot keep birds from flying over your head, but you can keep them from building a nest in your hair."

The hard decisions must be made before they have to be made.

If you want to keep yourself clean, you have to be prepared for the moment of temptation. The hard decisions must be made before they have to be made. Do not wait for the heat of temptation; decide now how you will respond when sin presents itself.

The life of purity does not happen on accident–it is chosen on purpose.

---

17 Hebrews 4:15

Remember that people can take everything from you except your integrity.

We live in a world where accusations and innuendo seem to rule the day, but even the "cancel culture" that is sweeping our generation cannot take your integrity. If you lose your integrity, it is because you gave it up. Potiphar's wife took Joseph's reputation temporarily but she could not rob him of his integrity. He lost his coat but kept his character.

No matter what you lose in life, do not lose the presence of God–the joy of walking with Jesus, the unbroken fellowship, and the wonder of living in His holiness with His touch on your life. Nothing is worth that. Do not trade it for anything.

The rest of Genesis 39 tells us of the false accusations made by Potiphar's wife that caused Joseph to be thrown in jail. But notice how the chapter ends in verses 21-23:

> *But the LORD was with Joseph, and shewed him mercy, and gave him favour in the sight of the*

keeper of the prison. And the keeper of the prison committed to Joseph's hand all the prisoners that were in the prison; and whatsoever they did there, he was the doer of it. The keeper of the prison looked not to any thing that was under his hand; because the LORD was with him, and that which he did, the LORD made it to prosper.

Don't miss the bookends to this part of Joseph's story. In the opening verses of the chapter, we read that God was with him. Now, we see the same thing at the end. Whether in the palace or the prison, the Lord was with him.

Whether you are up or down, whether people are for or against you, the one thing that cannot change in your life is the presence of God.

The record of the temptation of Jesus in Luke 4 is the perfect example of this principle. Verse 1 tells us He was *"led by the Spirit into the wilderness"* and verse 14 states that He *"returned in the power of the Spirit into Galilee."* Many people go into their wilderness filled with the Holy Spirit but do not come out that way. They walk with God for a season, but forget His goodness and their own weakness when temptation comes.

I can tell you on the authority of the Word of God that all of your life, you will face temptation. People think it will dissipate as they get older or move into different stages of life, but that is not the case. The flesh never stops, and religious flesh is still just flesh. It cannot be trusted.

Do you remember early in Joseph's story the first dream that God gave him? He saw himself as a sheaf that *"stood upright"* when his brothers' sheafs were bowing down to him.[18] Certainly that was prophetic of the day that his brothers would come and bow down before him in Egypt. But the only reason God put such honor upon him was because he was willing to live a life of honor. In every way, his life *"stood upright."* If you want God's best then you must choose to live a life of uprightness when others are bowing all around you.

There were three other men before Joseph of whom it was said in Genesis that the Lord was with them. They

---

18 Genesis 37:7

were his three immediate ancestors: Abraham,[19] Isaac,[20] and Jacob.[21] What a tremendous heritage of people living in God's presence! But it is not enough that others before us knew God and obeyed Him. In every generation, God is looking for individuals who will walk with Him, and through whom He can show Himself to others.

It is our turn. The Christian life is not history; it is present tense. This is not just for believers in previous times and other places. Determine that you will be one of those of whom it can be said today, *"The Lord was with them."*

---

19 Genesis 21:22
20 Genesis 26:24, 28
21 Genesis 28:15

Action Page

One truth...

You cannot avoid all temptation but you can endure temptation without sinning against God.

Memorize and Meditate...

"There hath no temptation taken you but such as is common to man: but God is faithful, who will not suffer you to be tempted above that ye are able; but will with the temptation also make a way to escape, that ye may be able to bear it." 1 Corinthians 10:13

Ask and Answer...

1. *How can memory be used to keep you from sin?*

2. *Which Bible character is a contrast to Joseph because he failed to acknowledge God's presence at the moment of temptation?*

Next Steps on My Journey...

Every person has their besetting sins. List the top three temptations which you have to fight. Then, find at least one Scripture that speaks to each of those areas. Write out the verses, commit them to memory, and quote them aloud when the temptation comes.

Serving the Lord in Your Difficulty

◇◇◇◇◇◇◇◇◇

Sometimes even when we do right it seems things turn out wrong. Perhaps you are trying to obey the Lord and honor God and you find yourself in less than desirable circumstances. Joseph understood that, and so does the Lord!

When Genesis chapter 39 ends, we find Joseph in jail, not for a crime, but for making a godly choice. Remember that the end of one chapter is never the end of the story. In verses 21 through 23, pay close attention to who was in that jail with him…

> *But the* Lord *was with Joseph, and shewed him mercy, and gave him favour in the sight of the keeper of the prison. And the keeper of the prison committed to Joseph's hand all the prisoners that were in the prison; and whatsoever they did there, he was the doer of it. The keeper of the prison looked not to any thing that was under his hand; because the* Lord *was with him, and that which he did, the* Lord *made it to prosper.*

Do you see the divine humor in this passage? Joseph was in jail, yet they put him in charge. They thought he did such good work that they left him alone and hardly even supervised him at all. After the unpleasant encounter with Potiphar's wife, he was once again in a place where God watched over him and gave him prosperity.

Yet he was still a prisoner.

People sometimes commit their life to Christ and imagine that there will be no difficulty with which to deal. If there is blessing, there will always be battles. In the oldest book in the Bible, we find a statement that has held true in every generation. Job 14:1 says, *"Man that is born of a woman is of few days and full of trouble."*

It is not going to be easy all the time. In fact, if you strive to follow Jesus Christ, you can count on the fact that there will be a war, because Satan opposes everything God ordains. If God is going to use you, bless your life, and work through you in the lives of other people, you can expect a level of opposition.[1]

We all can agree that we are living in difficult days. Everyone is having a hard time or struggling with something. There is stress and strain throughout life, and you are not going to avoid it. You must instead learn, by the grace of God, how to keep serving the Lord in the midst of it.

One of the great truths in Scripture is that victory is found, not after the battle, but in the middle of the battle. Peace is found, not after the storm subsides, but in the middle of the storm. You are not to serve the Lord only after circumstances have improved. You must serve Him while you are immersed in difficulty.

---

1   1 Peter 4:12-14

THE LORD WAS WITH JOSEPH

Pastor Clarence Sexton, under whom I served for many years, has had nearly a dozen spinal surgeries and a quadruple-bypass surgery. He moves more slowly than when I first met him, but he is still moving forward. He has been one of God's examples to me of persistence and perseverance.

"Scott," he said to me, "sometimes the most difficult thing to do in life is the only thing you can do."

"What is that?" I asked.

"Just keep putting one foot in front of the other."

William Carey, often called the pioneer of modern missions, said to his family before his death, "I hope somebody remembers that I was a plodder." It is not all excitement and adventure!

The people who found the journal of Christopher Columbus were so excited to read about his thrilling explorations. They found, on most pages, a simple three word entry: "We sailed on." You do not discover the New World every day! Some days you just keep sailing. The earlier in life you learn to keep serving the Lord in spite of the difficulty, the better off your whole life will be.

Often when journalists interview extremely elderly people, they ask them how they were able to endure so much in life. Almost without exception, every person I've heard has cited a realization that they could not change things or people around them but chose instead to just keep moving forward, and do what they could with what they had.

The only way you will be what God wants you to be is by serving Him in the midst of difficulty. For some insight on how to do that, we can once again follow the example of Joseph. What do you do when you don't know what to do and you don't know how it will turn out?

Do what you can where you are.

Some people miss the present by wishing for the future; they wait for things to get better and easier someday. The will of God begins by simply taking the next step.

You cannot back up to yesterday, and tomorrow may never get here. Someone observed, "Yesterday is a cancelled check, tomorrow is a promissory note, today is legal tender." The only day you have is today. We have no idea what is around the next bend or over the next horizon, but God has you in a particular place at this moment and you can serve Him right where you are. You cannot do everything, but you can do something.

Notice two key phrases. At the end of verse 22: "*... and whatsoever they did there, he was the doer of it.*" And at the end of verse 23: "*... and that which he did, the* LORD *made it to prosper.*" What a marvelous connection between our own responsibility and God's resources.

This passage shows us first what Joseph did, and then how God blessed it. D.L. Moody used to say that he wanted his life to be marked by: "My human best, filled with the Holy Spirit." It is not one or the other, but both. We are to do our best and let the Lord touch it as only He can.

The word *"whatsoever"* encompasses every area of life. It is not one part of your life that is to be given to God; it is every area.

"Whatsoever thy hand findeth to do, do it with thy might."[2]

"And whatsoever ye do in word or deed, do all in the name of the Lord Jesus, giving thanks to God and the Father by him."[3]

"And whatsoever ye do, do it heartily, as to the Lord, and not unto men."[4]

God has something different for every person. We are all to serve Him but not in the same way. My advice to you is simply to do what you can where you are.

We see in verse 21 that God showed Joseph mercy and gave him favor. Those are two wonderful words. If you want something to pray for every day of your life, pray that God will show you mercy and give you favor.

The Bible says in Lamentations 3:22-23, *"It is of the Lord's mercies that we are not consumed, because his compassions*

---

2   Ecclesiastes 9:10
3   Colossians 3:17
4   Colossians 3:23

fail not. They are new every morning: great is thy faithfulness." Aren't you glad for the fresh mercy of God today?

His mercy pertains to His relationship with you. His favor is for your relationship with everyone else. Every aspect of your life is in God's hands, and I have learned that if you will just do what He has given you to do, He will take care of the rest. He does the real work, and He will do more with your life in a moment than you can do in a lifetime, if you simply put it all in His hands.

The will of God is never future;
it is always present.

Too often we make the will of God far too complicated, usually because we are trying to figure out the future. The will of God is never future; it is always present. That is because He is a present-tense God. When Moses asked His name, He did not say, "I was" or "I will be." His answer was, "I AM."

It cannot get any clearer than Psalm 46:1. *"God is our refuge and strength, a very present help in trouble."* That means right where you are, God is working in you, for you, with you, and through you. Do what He has given you to do and trust Him for the rest.

A dear friend of mine who is now in Heaven was for many years a pastor in Alabama. His favorite message and life's motto was this: "Only God." How can you explain a life like that of Joseph? Only God. There is no other way.

How can you explain the blessing of God in any life? Do you think it has anything to do with us? Absolutely not. It is only God.

William Borden[5] died at 25 years of age while on his way to serve as a missionary to Muslim people in China. Perhaps you know his story, summarized in his own famous words: "No reserves. No retreats. No regrets." Inscribed on his tombstone in a cemetery in Cairo, Egypt it says: "Apart

---

5   One of my favorite biographies is the story of William Borden written by Mrs. Howard Taylor. *Borden of Yale* has been reprinted by Crown Christian Publications.

from faith in Christ, there is no explanation for such a life." Only God.

Understand that the blessing comes from God alone, and it comes as you do what He has given you to do.

Learn to minister to others who are having a hard time.

It is easy to allow even our Christian life to become very self-centered. When you learn to *"bear ye one another's burdens, and so fulfil the law of Christ,"*[6] it is an amazing thing to see how God begins to work in the midst of your burdens and battles.

The entirety of Genesis 40 is about Joseph's ministry to two fellow prisoners, the baker and the butler. In studying it so many times and focusing on the dream and its interpretation, I missed a key phrase in verse 4: *"And the captain of the guard charged Joseph with them, and he served them: and they continued a season in ward."* He

---

6   Galatians 6:2

served them! What a picture of Jesus, who was described in the Gospel records as a man who *"came not to be ministered unto, but to minister."*[7]

Joseph did not live morbidly introspective, trapped in his own feelings and challenges. *"And he asked Pharaoh's officers that were with him in the ward of his lord's house, saying, Wherefore look ye so sadly to day?"*[8] He was so interested in these two men that he recognized when their countenance had fallen and wanted to know what was wrong. He was not consumed with his own problems, but concerned instead about the needs of others.

The most miserable people on earth are those who are immersed in self-pity. The unhappiest people are the ones who are trying desperately to be happy. Those who learn the secret of true joy are those who know that it is not all about them; it is about pleasing God and ministering to the needs of those around them.

---

7   Matthew 20:28
8   Genesis 42:7

THE LORD WAS WITH JOSEPH

The Dead Sea is the lowest point on earth and a place where living organisms cannot survive. The reason for such death is that living water flows in but nothing ever flows out. God has designed that His children be tributaries and not depositories. When you minister to others, you stop being a "Dead Sea" Christian and start becoming a channel through which the Lord can bless others. When this becomes a reality, you will find that God works on both sides. A good example of this is seen in the suffering of another Old Testament character named Job. Do you remember when Job's situation changed? *"When he prayed for his friends."*[9]

In verse 8 they responded to Joseph's question, *"And they said unto him, We have dreamed a dream, and there is no interpreter of it. And Joseph said unto them, Do not interpretations belong to God? tell me them, I pray you."*

He did not ask about the dream first. Notice that his first question was not for information, but to share God's revelation. He wanted them to know the true and living

---

9   Job 42:10

God! Joseph spoke God's truth to these men who were pagans and idol worshippers. Speak in faith about the greatness of your God! Make much of the divine resources at our disposal. They are available even in the prison.

Others may not always remember your testimony, but God will. The story in Genesis 40 concluded with the baker dying and the butler forgetting about Joseph. But all was not in vain! God did not forget Joseph, and He has never forgotten you. His eye is on you, His ear is open to your prayer, and He has every hair on your head numbered. He is at work in your life. Allow Him to use you to minister to others.

Wait on God.

The next chapter begins this way: *"And it came to pass at the end of two full years, that Pharoah dreamed: and, behold, he stood by the river."*[10] We usually see this verse and keep right on reading, without fully appreciating the fact

---

10 Genesis 40:1

that so much time had passed after Joseph's encounter with the butler and the baker. Still in prison for a crime he did not commit, he just kept doing what he could do where he was for two full years.

If you are in such a place, trying to figure out what you are going to do–the best thing you can do is to simply wait quietly on the Lord.

From a human perspective it might be easy to say, "What a waste of time." God never wastes a single day when it is given to Him. The parentheses of life are a big part of the story; they often bring clarity to the whole story. You do not get the full picture until you see what God is doing during the in-between times in your life. If you are in such a place, trying to figure out what you are going to do–the best thing you can do is to simply wait quietly on the Lord. The most important lesson I had to learn in the greatest transition of my life was what it means to wait on God.

There is not much that is harder than this. Don't you hate sitting and waiting? I certainly do. We are probably the most impatient society in human history, getting fast food in a drive-thru and complaining that it isn't faster. We have high-speed Internet and get frustrated when the page does not load as fast as we want it to.

When I am flying, I dread hearing those words, "Ladies and gentlemen, we are in a holding pattern." The problem with a holding pattern is that you never have any idea how long you will be going around in circles. Everyone is in a hurry to get somewhere!

Have you ever wondered why Joshua and the children of Israel were called on to march around Jericho for seven days? They were commanded not to do or say anything during that time.[11] I'm sure many of them thought they were just walking around in circles for no good reason.

It was not some elite military strategy that sent them marching for a week. Their footsteps had no effect on the walls of that great city. God was not doing this to conquer

---

11 Joshua 6:1-26

Jericho; that was easy for Him. He was conquering Israel, teaching them to wait on Him and obey Him. That particular story ends with these words, *"So the Lord was with Joshua."*[12]

Time spent waiting on God is never wasted. While you are waiting, God is working in you and for you. Trust that in the silent periods of your life, He is at work.

We constantly emphasize service, but what did a servant in the Bible really do? He stood in a corner of the room with his eyes on the master and waited until the master called upon him to do something. The servant's number one job is not to serve, but to wait on the master.

If God says, "Move," you move. If He says, "Stop," you stop. Either way, it is not up to you but up to the Master.

The famed English author, John Milton observed: "They also serve who only stand and wait."[13] This line became a well-known slogan in England during the Second World War to emphasize that those who served at home were

---

12 Joshua 6:27
13 Taken from *Sonnet 19: When I Consider How My Light is Spent* by John Milton

just as needed as those who served abroad. Believers must remember that, in our lives, the assignments are left up to the Lord.

The story of Joseph is a point of reference throughout Scripture. In Psalm 105:17-22 we read:

> *He sent a man before them, even Joseph, who was sold for a servant: Whose feet they hurt with fetters: he was laid in iron: Until the time that his word came: the word of the LORD tried him. The king sent and loosed him; even the ruler of the people, and let him go free. He made him lord of his house, and ruler of all his substance: To bind his princes at his pleasure; and teach his senators wisdom.*

God's purpose. God's time. God's Word. The Lord has a plan in every difficulty we face. Remember that with one word from Him, everything changes. Until that time comes in your life, rest in His promises and wait on the Lord.

"I had fainted, unless I had believed to see the goodness of the LORD in the land of the living. Wait on the LORD: be

of good courage, and he shall strengthen thine heart: wait, I say on the LORD."[14]

From a human perspective, Genesis 41:14 is the great turning point in the life of Joseph: "*Then Pharaoh sent and called Joseph, and they brought him hastily out of the dungeon: and he shaved himself, and changed his raiment, and came in unto Pharaoh.*" He had to be prepared physically to meet the ruler of Egypt, but spiritually he was ready.

If you are in a waiting period, stay as close to God as possible. Be as thoroughly right with Him as you can be, so at the moment of clarity you will be ready for whatever God has for you to do.

"*And Pharaoh said unto Joseph, I have dreamed a dream, and there is none that can interpret it: and I have heard say of thee, that thou canst understand a dream to interpret it. And Joseph answered Pharaoh, saying, It is not in me: God shall give Pharaoh an answer of peace.*"[15]

---

14 Psalm 27:13-14
15 Genesis 41:15-16

Joseph did not strut into the palace and say, "Yes, I am the best dream interpreter in the land. It's a good thing you heard about me." Instead, he told Pharaoh who would ultimately make the meaning of the dream known. He pointed Pharoah to the God who had been with him at every season of his own life.

This was his big break! His golden opportunity! But his first words were: *"It is not in me: God shall…"* The New Testament parallel to this statement is Galatians 2:20: *"I am crucified with Christ: nevertheless I live; yet not I, but Christ liveth in me."* Not I, but Christ. Not me, but God. Joseph's response was full of faith and humility. He was a man who, during the waiting process, stayed close to God so that he was prepared when the door was opened and a way was made for him. Do not allow your trouble to become a wedge that divides you from God; let it be a prod to drive you nearer to Him.

Refuse to get stuck in your past.

We began our study of Joseph by learning how to see God in our past. At any point in his life, Joseph could have been so discouraged by circumstances, disillusioned by people, or distracted by his own thoughts, that he would have been unable to move forward. At many junctures on life's journey, you will have to choose to move past your past. How did Joseph keep serving the Lord in the midst of difficulty?

> *And unto Joseph were born two sons before the years of famine came, which Asenath the daughter of Potipherah priest of On bare unto him. And Joseph called the name of the firstborn Manasseh: For God, said he, hath made me forget all my toil, and all my father's house. And the name of the second called he Ephraim: For God hath caused me to be fruitful in the land of my affliction.*[16]

God gave Joseph two sons during this stage of his life. Children are always God's gift,[17] and they have a way of

16 Genesis 41:50-52
17 Genesis 4:1; Psalm 127:3

helping you concentrate on the future. He named his children Manasseh, which meant "forgetting," and Ephraim, which meant "fruitful." In ancient civilization, names were chosen carefully, and carried with them a great deal of meaning. Mark the words *"forget"* in verse 51 and *"fruitful"* in verse 52. There is a divine order here. The first was a reference to his past, the second to his future.

Hebrews 12:15 warns against *"any root of bitterness."* No good fruit grows in the garden of bitterness. Only as we choose to forget will we be able to bear fruit.

Manasseh was a symbol that God had helped Joseph move on from his past. You cannot move forward for God until you deal with your past.

Ephraim represented how fruitful his life had become because he continued to believe God had much more in store for him. We must do the same.

"But the path of the just is as the shining light, that shineth more and more unto the perfect day."[18]

---

18 Proverbs 4:18

"Call unto me, and I will answer thee, and show thee great and mighty things, which thou knowest not."[19]

"Now unto him that is able to do exceeding abundantly above all that we ask or think, according to the power that worketh in us."[20]

---

*One key to moving beyond the past
is learning to forgive.*

These passages do not suggest that you have never been wronged or that you have never done wrong. They simply tell us that God will make everything right in the end. He has more for His servants.

Do you know where we all seem to get stuck? At the last place where we refused to trust and obey God. Some people get stuck early in life and they live in that rut for the rest of their lives. Vance Havner said, "A rut is just a

---

19 Jeremiah 33:3
20 Ephesians 3:20

grave with both ends knocked out." They may live another 60 years, but they die before they die, missing so much that God had for them.

Hudson Taylor said, "God is always advancing." Are you going to move forward with Him?

Forgive.

One key to moving beyond the past is learning to forgive. The second half of Joseph's story, found in Genesis 42-47, is a beautiful story of forgiveness and restoration.

It is possible that the circumstances may get better, but the root of bitterness could remain. Joseph rose to a level where he could have anything he wanted, but if he allowed bitterness to take over regarding what had happened to him before, he would never have been a blessing. To have the blessing, you must be a blessing. That can only happen by keeping bitterness out of your life.

Look at one snapshot of Joseph's life in Genesis 45:4-8, as he revealed himself to his brothers:

THE LORD WAS WITH JOSEPH

And Joseph said unto his brethren, Come near to me, I pray you. And they came near. And he said, I am Joseph your brother, whom ye sold into Egypt. Now therefore be not grieved, nor angry with yourselves, that ye sold me hither: for God did send me before you to preserve life. For these two years hath the famine been in the land: and yet there are five years, in the which there shall neither be earing nor harvest. And God sent me before you to preserve you a posterity in the earth, and to save your lives by a great deliverance. So now it was not you that sent me hither, but God: and he hath made me a father to Pharaoh, and lord of all his house, and a ruler throughout all the land of Egypt.

He mentioned God three times in these few verses. We all live with either a Godward view or a manward view of life. God is greater! The secret to forgiving others is to stop concentrating on them and begin to concentrate on Him. After all, He has forgiven us immeasurably. Considering how He has treated us—hell-deserving sinners, graciously forgiven–can we possibly justify holding on to whatever we think someone else has done to us?

"And be ye kind one to another, tenderhearted, forgiving one another, even as God for Christ's sake hath forgiven you."[21]

"Forbearing one another, and forgiving one another, if any man have a quarrel against any: even as Christ forgave you, so also do ye."[22]

You may recall earlier in this story an episode in which Joseph's brothers paid him for the food they were taking back home, but he had his servants put the money back without their knowledge. It is a beautiful picture of forgiveness, because it shows a man who wants nothing from them but only wishes to give to them.

The greatest giving is forgiving. In fact, the very word *"forgive"* contains "give" in it. The greatest gift you can give anyone is what Jesus gave you, and that is forgiveness.[23]

---

21 Ephesians 4:32
22 Colossians 3:13
23 Matthew 18:21-35

THE LORD WAS WITH JOSEPH

Joseph's brothers would bring up their previous failures later in life, but Joseph never did. Forgiveness doesn't mean that you have amnesia–it means that you choose never to bring it up again. The power to forgive comes from looking beyond others and seeing the Lord. In the words of Joseph, *"ye thought evil against me; but God meant it unto good."*[24]

Joseph's difficulty became the platform from which his family and everyone else in the nation had their needs met in a time of famine. God may be getting ready to use you, and whatever difficulty you are in right now to meet not only your own needs but those of others.

As Joseph's father was dying he gave a prophecy about Joseph's future. In Genesis 49:22, he predicted that Joseph would be like the *"fruitful bough"* of a tree *"whose branches run over the wall."* Although obstacles would stand in his way none of that would stop God's fruitful work in him. Because his roots went deeply into God's resources, his life would grow to feed many others.

---

24 Genesis 50:20

THE LORD WAS WITH JOSEPH

Take the time to read the entire passage, Genesis 49:22-26, and observe both the battles and blessings in Joseph's life. They always go together. In the midst of the section there is a beautiful reference to the coming Messiah, the *"shepherd"* and the *"stone"*.[25] The Lord Jesus always shows His tenderness and strength in the middle of our difficulty. It has been said, "When Jesus is all you have, you discover that He is all you need!"

The final words of Jacob to Joseph promised that the blessing of God would be on *"him that was separate from his brethren."*[26] This truly was the story of Joseph's life. He had been separated geographically and circumstantially from his brothers. But there was more—he was spiritually set apart from his brothers. *"The Lord was with him."*

Refuse to be sidetracked or distracted. Keep serving the Lord. He is with you.

---

25 Genesis 49:24
26 Genesis 49:26

Action Page

One truth...

There is no shortcut to God's best and there is no substitute for faithfulness.

Memorize and Meditate...

"My brethren, count it all joy when ye fall into divers temptations; knowing this, that the trying of your faith worketh patience. But let patience have her perfect work, that ye may be perfect and entire, wanting nothing." James 1:2-4

Ask and Answer...

1. *What is one example of Joseph's faithfulness in the middle of difficult circumstances?*

2. *Why is waiting on God so hard and yet so important?*

Next Steps on My Journey...

When we are dealing with difficulties, it is very easy to become self-centered. Identify someone else this week who is struggling in some way and show the love of Christ to them. Write a letter, make a call or visit. Do something to encourage another person.

Trusting the Lord for Your Future

◇◇◇◇◇◇◇◇◇◇

Life is a story, and in many ways, it is made up of chapters. *"We spend our years as a tale that is told."*[1] Like any book, all of the chapters are not the same length and not every chapter is as enjoyable as others. I try to write in a journal each day. It has been a good way for me to remember the things God is teaching me and to record what He is doing in my life. One day as I flipped through my journal, I came to a blank page and wondered what would be on that page. Only the Lord knows. Yet I know that the same One who

---

1   Psalm 90:9

has guided and guarded my life to this point is the One holding the pen for the unwritten days.

The Bible speaks of the times of our life being divided into seasons. *"To every thing there is a season, and a time to every purpose under the heaven."*[2] Not every season may be your favorite, but all of them are important. In every natural season on this planet, God is getting it ready for the next one. The same is true with your life.

Genesis 50 is not only the final chapter of that book but the final chapter of Joseph's life. He is described here as an old man, which is strange for me, because I always see him frozen in time, in my mind, as that 17-year-old young man wearing his father's coat. But none of us stay young forever.

Old age is relative depending on how old you are, but it is eventually a reality that none of us can escape. Life moves on. That is why you should not wish your life away. Some people, especially in their youth, wish they could skip a particular season of life, and they miss what God has for them in that season.

---

2   Ecclesiastes 3:1

When I was in junior high school, I wanted to be in high school. When I was in high school, I wanted to get my driver's license. Then I wanted to be out of high school and in college. Once in college, I wanted to be out. Then I wanted to be married and have children. Once the children arrived, I suddenly wanted everything to slow down. But it doesn't work that way. Life seems to pick up speed as it moves forward.

Charles Spurgeon said that the way to make the most of your life is to meditate on your death. What he meant was that you should go to the end of your life, find out what is most important at that point, and work your way backward. What do you want for your future? You are choosing that right now.

People say they are trusting Christ for their eternal salvation but then refuse to trust Him for their present situation. Four times in Scripture we are told that *"the just shall live by faith."*[3] Faith is not only how you come to Christ, it is how you are to follow Him every day. The Christian life

---

3   Habakkuk 2:4; Romans 1:17; Galatians 3:11; Hebrews 10:38

is a faith life. Rest in the fact that God has worked in your past, believe that He is enabling you for what you must do today, and trust that your future is in His hands.

The final verse of Genesis, verse 26 of chapter 50, says, *"So Joseph died, being an hundred and ten years old: and they embalmed him, and he was put in a coffin in Egypt."*

This description of Joseph could be applied to all of us eventually, because death is inevitable if the Lord tarries His coming. In the very familiar words of Hebrews 9:27, *"And as it is appointed unto men once to die, but after this the judgment."*

The biggest day of your life will not be graduation, your wedding day, or retirement–it will be the day you see God! We are all getting ready to meet the Lord face to face.

Death is not an end, but a doorway, a bridge into eternity. For a Christian, it will be the most wonderful day ever as you see Jesus Christ for the first time. Yes, we have much to look forward to.

When you see Him and kneel at His nail-pierced feet at the Judgment Seat of Christ, some things are simply not going to matter and other things will matter a great deal. Live for that day. What matters in eternity should be what matters most today.

As a young man, I became fascinated by the epitaphs that people choose to put on grave markers. I have collected dozens of them, including famous ones from all over the country. My personal favorite is the unusual epitaph of a man named Solomon Peas:

> Beneath these clouds and beneath these trees
> Lies the body of Solomon Peas.
> This isn't Peas–it's just the pod.
> Peas shelled out and went to God.

Some day we will all shell out and go home to God! When that day comes for you, how would you like to be remembered?

As we walk through Genesis 50, we come to the conclusion that Joseph finished strong. So many people start well, but do not end well. I have taken Acts 20:24 as my life verse: *"But none of these things move me, neither count I my life dear unto myself, so that I might finish my course with joy, and the ministry, which I have received of the Lord Jesus, to testify the gospel of the grace of God.*" More than anything, I want to finish my life well with the Lord!

I have no idea how much time I have left, but I want to trust God for my future and I want all He has for me. How do we go about doing that? Let's follow Joseph's pattern.

Honor those who instructed you.

The first 13 verses of Genesis 50 are about the death of Joseph's father, Jacob, and how his son honored him at that time. We know all too well that Jacob was not a perfect man, but we should also consider that the foundation for everything Joseph knew about God was instilled in him by his father during the first 17 years of life.

We do not read in Genesis 50 of Joseph criticizing Jacob or talking about what he failed to do for him. This passage is about a man who chose to honor his father.

We live in a society that picks people apart with regularity, and many young people only want to criticize those who went before them. Remember that if it weren't for the previous generation, we would not even be here. Someday your children will recognize the flaws in your life, so I would suggest we stop expecting perfection from one another and give honor where it is due. If you want God to bless your future, you should not forget your past.

"Remember the days of old, consider the years of many generations: ask thy father, and he will shew thee; thy elders, and they will tell thee."[4]

Go back and read Genesis 48-49. You will see that Joseph sought counsel from his elderly father. That is such a wise thing to do. I am amazed by how many people prepare for the biggest decisions of life by seeking counsel from their peers, who have no more life experience than they do. Find spiritual people, mature believers, who have been down the road further than you have, and seek counsel from them.

Others have invested in you to get you to this point. Do not betray the trust you have been given or waste the stewardship God has put in your hands. Life is a relay race;

---

4   Deuteronomy 32:7

you have been handed the baton to both carry for a season and then pass it on someday. By the grace of God, honor those whom the Lord has brought into your life.

Leave all of the details of life in God's hands.

From start to finish, it seems that Joseph left the big decisions and direction of his life up to God. Jim Elliot once said, "God always gives His best to those who leave the choice with Him." We make terrible mistakes…God never does. He is God and we are not.

There is no such thing as a "self-made man." According to Psalm 100:3, *"Know ye that the Lord he is God: it is he that hath made us, and not we ourselves; we are his people, and the sheep of his pasture."* Joseph was well aware that God had ordered the steps and the detours of his life.

Not all people live this way:

> *And Joseph returned into Egypt, he, and his brethren, and all that went up with him to bury*

> *his father, after he had buried his father. And*
> *when Joseph's brethren saw that their father was*
> *dead, they said, Joseph will peradventure hate*
> *us, and will certainly requite us all the evil which*
> *we did unto him.*[5]

How interesting that, after Joseph forgave his brothers and took care of them for many years, they would still think that he would seek revenge. It reveals their own fleshly hearts and their failure to understand what God had done in Joseph's heart. Joseph was walking in the Spirit, not the flesh.

The story continues:

> *And they sent a messenger unto Joseph, saying,*
> *Thy father did command before he died, saying,*
> *So shall ye say unto Joseph, Forgive, I pray thee*
> *now, the trespass of thy brethren, and their sin;*
> *for they did unto thee evil: and now, we pray*
> *thee, forgive the trespass of the servants of the*

---

5   Genesis 50:14-15

THE LORD WAS WITH JOSEPH

God of thy father. And Joseph wept when they spake unto him.[6]

There is no record that Jacob had ever said such a thing. The brothers missed the fact that their protection was not because of their earthly father but because of the Heavenly Father. Joseph's tender response shows that he kept a right spirit to the end. In a harsh world it is easy to develop a hard heart. We all begin with the innocence and idealism of youth, and if we are not careful we can become cynical and sour with age. Ask the Lord to help you stay tender toward God and others.

And his brethren also went and fell down before his face; and they said, Behold, we be thy servants. And Joseph said unto them, Fear not: for am I in the place of God? But as for you, ye thought evil against me; but God meant it unto good, to bring to pass, as it is this day, to save much people alive.[7]

---

6 Genesis 50:16-17
7 Genesis 50:18-20

Joseph did not want them as servants. They were his brothers. He would never think of doing something that suggested he was acting as God toward them. This was a man who left both the good and bad of his life in God's hands. He was not concerned with seeking vengeance for himself. Because of that, he put his own life and that of his brothers back in the Lord's hands, believing that He would do right.

You will see, hear, and experience some things now that do not make much sense, but one day you will look back and see that God was working in those very things. When you cannot wrap your mind around all of it, just say, "Lord, I don't understand it all but I am leaving my life up to You."

The Lord was with Joseph all the way to the end. Wouldn't you like that for your own life?

Love and lift up others.

Instead of getting payback like his brothers thought he would do, he did the exact opposite! We read in verses 21-22: *"Now therefore fear ye not: I will nourish you, and your little ones. And he comforted them, and spake kindly unto them. And Joseph dwelt in Egypt, he, and his father's house: and Joseph lived an hundred and ten years."*

This passage shows three specific ways he ministered to them. He provided for them physically (*"nourish"*), ministered to them spiritually (*"comforted"*), and simply showed kindness to them (*"spake kindly"*).

Would God that we had more people who just nourished, comforted and spoke kindly. The world is getting more rude, more crude, and more ugly with every passing day. Amid all of the fussing and fighting, I will remind you that the mark of a Christian is supposed to be the act of showing love to each other.[8] In this way, and so many others, Joseph is a beautiful picture and type of Christ.

If you can learn to leave your life in God's hands, you can minister to other people because you do not see a need to try to right every wrong. You can trust Him to do that. If you want God's continued blessing, seek to be a blessing to other people.

---

8   John 13:35

Stay in God's Word and use your words to share it with others.

It is beautiful to see how the entire story ends in Genesis 50:23-26.

> *And Joseph saw Ephraim's children of the third generation: the children also of Machir the son of Manasseh were brought up upon Joseph's knees. And Joseph said unto his brethren, I die: and God will surely visit you, and bring you out of this land unto the land which he sware to Abraham, to Isaac, and to Jacob. And Joseph took an oath of the children of Israel, saying, God will surely visit you, and ye shall carry up my bones from hence. So Joseph died, being an hundred and ten years old: and they embalmed him, and he was put in a coffin in Egypt.*

When Joseph was nearing the end of his life, he still meditated on the faithfulness and the promises of God. He had his share of disappointments in life and I'm sure he was disillusioned with people from time to time. Those closest to him hurt him and let him down. But he ended on a happy note as he recalled what the Lord had promised to his predecessors.

Do you want your faith to grow? Live in the Word. *"So then faith cometh by hearing, and hearing by the word of God."*[9] Read the scriptures. Pray your way through passages. Meditate on the Word of God. Study it. God has so much He wants to say to you that will help to grow your faith.

As an old man, after decades of overseeing the care of thousands of orphans and seeing the Lord provide millions of dollars to help accomplish that task, George Mueller was told, "You seem like a happy man. How have you stayed so happy?" "I am a happy man," he answered, throwing back his head in laughter. "Happy, happy, happy." "How did you do it?" "Every day, before doing anything else, I opened my Bible and got my soul happy in Jesus." The old man struggled to get down on his knees, but he laid his open Bible on the floor and got down behind it. He put his finger on a verse and looked up to Heaven. "Every morning I read

---

9   Romans 10:17

my Bible until I found one of God's promises," he explained. "Then I looked up to Heaven and said, 'Lord, you promised and I am claiming this one today.'" Mueller said there was not a single day that God did not keep His Word. If you want to finish with joy then you must finish in faith.

Do you want your faith to grow? Live in the Word. Read the scriptures. Pray your way through passages. Meditate on the Word of God. Study it.

People tend to start excitedly with all of the dreams of life, but so many eventually become bitter old people. Things may not turn out the way you thought they would, and people often will fail to do right. You will even disappoint yourself! We must keep our eyes on our perfect, unchanging Lord, and the only way to do that is to live in the Word of God.

Joseph not only personalized God's promises, he communicated them to others around him. In two consecutive verses, he uttered the same exact phrase: *"God will surely visit you."* God will! Speak with certainty and confidence in God. How great it would be for each of us to end this race with an exclamation point and not a question mark. You will find that the older you get, the less confidence you will have in yourself. You actually know more than when you were younger but you begin to realize how little you know.

Joseph's confidence was not in himself but in God. You can finish well despite any perceived shortcoming if you lean on the Lord and put your confidence in Him. There is nothing greater for you to leave behind than a clear testimony of faith in God. Use your influence to share the goodness of God.

Millions of people in our world right now are living every day in depression and despair. They need to meet some people who are speaking out of faith in God. It is time for God's people, young and old alike, to get their eyes back on Him. Only then can we point others to Him.

Genesis 50 began by focusing on Joseph's relationship with those who came before him. It ends with a look at those who came after him. Abraham, Isaac, Jacob, Joseph, the children of Israel. The story goes on and on. You are a link in a very long chain. Someone paid the price, loved you to the Lord, taught you the truth, invested in you and influenced you so that you would have the opportunity to come to Him.

Now it is your turn. Trust God for your future.

One beautiful summer afternoon in north Georgia where I was preaching, I decided to take a run. As I got to the outskirts of the small town where I was staying, I encountered an old Civil War cemetery. I am an avid student of history, so I could not resist the chance to veer off the road and take a look.

There were many interesting markers to see, but one stood out as the largest by far. I was certain this must represent someone very important, and upon further inspection I was proven correct.

THE LORD WAS WITH JOSEPH

It was not an army officer or battle hero, but a wife and mother. The marker included her name, birth date and death date, with that dash in between that represented a great deal of living. But the one line epitaph was one of the most powerful I have ever seen. It simply read: "She lived and died as a Christian."

I pray that my memorial can read like that. Everyone wants to die as a Christian, but not everyone wants to live like a Christian.

If you want to be prepared for that day when you see Jesus face to face for the first time–start today, and live every day obeying and trusting in Him. You don't know where or when you will die, but you can choose how you will die.

It is up to you to decide if you will finish in faith. The Lord is with you, and you will be with Him soon.

Action Page

One truth...

God is already in your future and He will meet you as you continue to walk by faith.

Memorize and Meditate...

"But seek ye first the kingdom of God, and his righteousness; and all these things shall be added unto you. Take therefore no thought for the morrow: for the morrow shall take thought for the things of itself. Sufficient unto the day is the evil thereof." Matthew 6:33-34

Ask and Answer...

1. *In what ways did Joseph seek to pass on faith and hope to those coming behind him?*

2. *How were Joseph's final words a statement of faith for the future?*

Next Steps on My Journey...

Reach out to two individuals who have been an encouragement, mentor, or good example to you. Let them know how much you appreciate their influence on your life. Ask them to continue to pray for you, and if needed, seek counsel regarding any coming decisions.

Afterword

The last words of Genesis 50 are these: *"So Joseph died, being an hundred and ten years old: and they embalmed him, and he was put in a coffin in Egypt."* But is that where Joseph is now?

His body was buried, but Joseph went to be with God. Think of this! God comes to be with us in this life and then we go to be with Him for all of eternity.

"Then shall the dust return to the earth as it was: and the spirit shall return unto God who gave it."[1]

---

1   Ecclesiastes 12:7

"We are confident, I say, and willing rather to be absent from the body, and to be present with the Lord."[2]

Joseph is still very much alive–more alive than ever! And he is no longer dealing with persecution, temptation, or opposition. There is no joy like belonging to the Lord. He comes to live in our heart the moment we receive Christ as Savior and then we go to live in His house for eternity. His presence gives us God's best in both worlds. *"Surely goodness and mercy shall follow me all the days of my life: and I will dwell in the house of the LORD for ever."*[3]

Every believer's story ends at the throne of God. We will be with Him and He will be with us for eternity. In the last book of the Bible, we find a description of the final destination of the believer:

"And I heard a great voice out of heaven saying, Behold, the tabernacle of God is with men, and he will dwell with them, and they shall be his people, and God himself shall be with them, and be their God."[4]

---

2   2 Corinthians 5:8
3   Psalm 23:6
4   Revelation 21:3

Live in His presence today and look forward to the day that you will be in His presence forever.

Use the following appendices as resources for further study. You may want to give the next month to continued meditation on the life of Joseph and the presence of God in your own life.

A Month through the Life of Joseph

◇◇◇◇◇◇◇◇◇

It is exciting to see Joseph in so many contexts and connected to so many different people, yet always living in the presence of the Lord. Follow Joseph through different locations, circumstances, and relationships and you will see that the constant of his life was his unchanging God.

- Genesis 37:1-11–Joseph and His Dreams
- Genesis 37:12-27–Joseph and His Betrayal
- Genesis 37:28-36–Joseph and the Midianites

THE LORD WAS WITH JOSEPH

- Genesis 39:1-6–Joseph and Potiphar
- Genesis 39:7-12–Joseph and His Temptation
- Genesis 39:13-23–Joseph and the Prison
- Genesis 40:1-23–Joseph and the Butler and Baker
- Genesis 41:1-16–Joseph and Pharoah
- Genesis 41:17-38–Joseph and the Interpretation
- Genesis 41:39-49–Joseph and Egypt
- Genesis 41:50-57–Joseph and His Children
- Genesis 42:1-17–Joseph and His Family
- Genesis 42:18-38–Joseph and His Secret
- Genesis 43:1-15–Joseph and His Brothers
- Genesis 43:16-34–Joseph and His Kindness
- Genesis 44:1-45:2–Joseph and the Revelation
- Genesis 45:3-15–Joseph and His Forgiveness
- Genesis 45:16-46:27–Joseph and the Children of Israel
- Genesis 46:28-47:12–Joseph and His Father
- Genesis 47:13-27–Joseph and the Famine
- Genesis 47:28-48:22–Joseph and the Blessing
- Genesis 49:22-26–Joseph and the Future
- Genesis 50:1-13–Joseph and His Mourning

THE LORD WAS WITH JOSEPH

- Genesis 50:14-21–Joseph and His Humility
- Genesis 50:22-26–Joseph and His Last Days
- Exodus 13:19; Joshua 24:32–Joseph and His Bones
- Deuteronomy 33:13-17; Judges 1:22–Joseph and His Descendants
- Psalm 105:16-23–Joseph and His Testimony
- Acts 7:9-18–Joseph and God's Plan
- Hebrews 11:22–Joseph and His Faith

30 Days in God's Presence

This is not the end of the subject—there is no end to the presence of the Lord! It is impossible to exhaust our infinite God. My prayer is that this little book will encourage you to continue seeking the Lord and following Him. In addition to the many Scriptures referenced throughout the preceding pages, the following verses in both the Old and New Testaments have been selected to help you continue your study of the presence of God.

Meditate on one of the following passages each day over the next month. Each prayer, promise, and principle will help you to be more conscious of God's presence. God is the all-present God and very present with His people. We must seek each day to live in the light of His presence.

☐ Genesis 28:10-22

☐ Exodus 33:12-23

☐ Deuteronomy 31:6-8

☐ Joshua 1:8-9

☐ Psalm 15:1-5

☐ Psalm 16:11

☐ Psalm 23:1-6

☐ Psalm 27:1-14

☐ Psalm 46:1-11

☐ Psalm 73:1-28

☐ Psalm 95:1-2

☐ Psalm 100:1-5

☐ Psalm 139:1-24

☐ Isaiah 57:15

☐ Jeremiah 23:23-24

☐ Jeremiah 29:11-13

☐ Jonah 1:1-10; 2:1-10

☐ Matthew 18:18-20

☐ Matthew 28:19-20

☐ John 1:14-18

☐ John 14:16-27

☐ John 15:1-7

☐ Acts 3:13-21

☐ Acts 17:24-31

☐ 1 Corinthians 3:16-17

☐ Hebrews 4:14-16

☐ Hebrews 10:19-22

☐ Hebrews 13:5-6

☐ James 4:6-10

☐ 1 John 4:12-16

Joseph as a Type of Christ

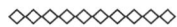

Joseph is one of the few people in Scripture of whom nothing evil is said. This does not mean that he was not a sinner, but rather that the Holy Spirit chose to emphasize only the positive example of his life. I believe one reason for this is that Joseph is one of the most beautiful types of Christ in the Old Testament. His life, in so many ways, paralleled and foreshadowed the greater Deliverer that was to come–the Lord Jesus Christ.

The following is adapted from numerous sources which have pointed out the amazing comparisons between the life of Joseph and the life of Jesus.

Joseph: The Son

- Beloved of the Father–Genesis 37:3 (Matthew 3:17)
- Shepherd–Genesis 37:2 (John 10:11-14)
- Hated by the brethren–Genesis 37:4-5, 8 (John 15:25)
- They would not believe–Genesis 37:5 (John 7:5)
- A true witness–Genesis 37:2 (John 7:7)
- Envied–Genesis 37:11 (Mark 15:10, Matthew 27:17,18)
- Sent unto the brethren–Genesis 37:13 (Luke 20:13, Heb. 10:7)
- From Hebron–Genesis 37:14 (John 17:5, 24)
- Conspired Against–Genesis 37:18 (Matthew 27:1, John 11:53)
- Bargained for–Genesis 37:26, 27 (Mark 14:10)

- Stripped–Genesis 37:23 (Matthew 27:28, John 19:23)
- Sat and watched–Genesis 37:25 (Matthew 27:36)
- Sold for a slave–Genesis 37:28 (Matthew 26:15)
- Taken to Egypt–Genesis 37:38 (Matthew 2:14-15)

Joseph: The Servant

- God was with him–Genesis 39:2, 21, 23 (John 16:32)
- Prospered–Genesis 39:2, 3 (Isaiah 53:10)
- All in his hand–Genesis 39:4, 8 (John 3:35)
- Pleased the master–Genesis 39:4, 8 (John 3:35)
- Tempted–Genesis 39:7 (Matthew 4)
- Falsely accused–Genesis 39:16-18 (Matthew 26:59-60)
- Bound–Genesis 39:20 (Matthew 27:2)
- Offered no defense–Genesis 39:20 (Isaiah 53:7)
- Two other prisoners / one saved, one lost–Genesis 40:2, 3 (Luke 23:32)

- Suffered under Gentiles–Egypt–Genesis 39:1, 20 (Acts 4:26-27)
- Respected by jailer–Genesis 39:21 (Luke 23:47)

Joseph: The Sovereign

- Taken from the dungeon–Genesis 41:14 (Revelation 1:18)
- Loosed bonds–Psalm 105:20 (Acts 2:24)
- Changed clothes–Genesis 41:14 (John 20:6-7)
- Spirit in him–Genesis 41:38 (Acts 10:38)
- Had God's wisdom–Genesis 41:39 (John 5:20, Matthew 13:54)
- Ruled over the house–Genesis 41:40 (Hebrews 3:6)
- Rules all the people–Genesis 41:40 (Acts 5:31)
- Shared throne–Genesis 41:42-43 (Revelation 3:21)
- Nothing done without him–Genesis 41:44 (John 15:5)
- Men bowed to him–Genesis 41:43 (Philippians 2:10)

- Given a new name–Genesis 41:45 (Philippians 2:9-10)
- 30 Years old–Genesis 41:46 (Luke 3:23)
- Gentile bride–Genesis 41:45 (Ephesians 5:25-27)
- Do what he says–Genesis 41:57 (John 2:5)
- All nations come–Genesis 41:57 (Isaiah 49:6)
- Sovereignty–Genesis 37:5-10 (Matthew 28:19-20)

Joseph: The Savior

- They knew him not–Genesis 42:8 (John 1:10-11; Acts 3:17)
- Guilty of his blood–Genesis 42:21-22 (Matthew 27:25)
- He wept–Genesis 42:24 (Luke 19:41)
- Punished them–Genesis 42:7, 17 (Hosea 9:17)
- Confessed guilt–Genesis 44:16 (Hosea 5:15)
- Revealed the second time–Genesis 45:1 (Acts 7:13; Zechariah 12:10)
- Troubled–Genesis 45:3 (Zechariah 12:10)
- God did it–Genesis 45:8 (Acts 2:23)

THE LORD WAS WITH JOSEPH

- Behold, me–Genesis 45:12 (Luke 24:29)
- Shewed grace–Genesis 45:4-15 (Isaiah 54:7-8)
- Glory revealed–Genesis 45:13 (Luke 24:26)
- Brethren carried the message–Genesis 45:9-10 (Mark 16:15)
- Invited to come–Genesis 45:18, 19 (Matthew 11:28-30)
- Comforted them–Genesis 50:21 (Isaiah 40:1-2)
- Supplied their need–Genesis 45:20 (Isaiah 2:1-5)

Recommended Resources

for Further Reading
on the Life of Joseph

God Built by Steve Farrar

Joseph: God's Man in Egypt by Leslie Flynn

Representative Men of the Bible by George Matheson

Joseph by F.B. Meyer

The Life of Joseph by Clarence Sexton

History Makers of the Old Testament by Elmer Towns

Bible Characters by Alexander Whyte

Our desire is to provide gospel and revival resources as inexpensively as possible to as many people as possible. In order to do this, we depend on generous gifts from friends like you.

If this book has been a help to you, please consider giving to extend the ministry to others. Your gift is tax-deductible and will be used to help many hear the truth of Jesus Christ. You may invest securely online at:

enjoyingthejourney.org/joseph
Following God's Word · Finding Christ's Joy

Thank you for your prayers and support.

- **Hear** full-length messages on the life of Joseph at youtube.com/drscottpauley.
- **Obtain** the digital version of this book at no cost through iBooks or Kindle.
- **Visit** our online Bible study library at enjoyingthejourney.org/joseph to access the audiobook, obtain series graphics, and download companion study sheets for use in small-group Bible studies, Sunday School classes, or personal discipleship.

  Bulk pricing for the book is available for multiple copies.

enjoyingthejourney.org/joseph
Following God's Word · Finding Christ's Joy

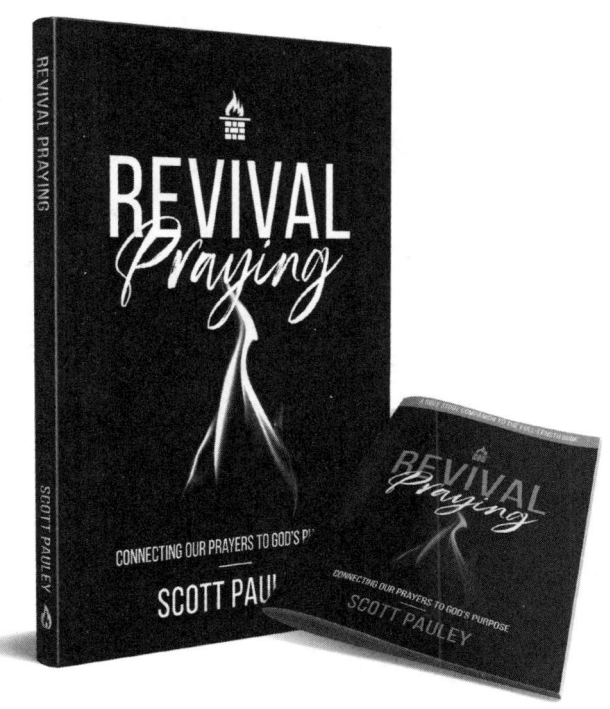

Enjoying the Journey

Life is a short trip to somewhere forever!
How will you make the trip?

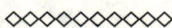

We live in a mobile society and it seems that everyone is in a hurry to get where they are going! Life itself is a journey and all of us are headed somewhere forever. An all-wise God has designed it so that those who follow His way can enjoy Heaven someday and also enjoy the journey today. The Bible, God's Word to man, is the roadmap for time and eternity.

✝ Begin by determining your destination.

Every journey begins by settling where you are going. Without direction, we all just wander aimlessly through life, searching for meaning and purpose. Thousands of years ago a prophet named Isaiah wrote, *"All we like sheep have gone astray; we have turned every one to his own way; and the Lord hath laid on him the iniquity of us all."*[1] Some things never change!

"For all have sinned and come short of the glory of God."[2] On our own we all go away from God. This is why Jesus Christ came: to take our sin and give us His salvation. Only He can return us to the path we were created to walk and bring us to God. Jesus said, *"I am the way, the truth, and the life: no man cometh unto the Father, but by me."*[3]

Jesus Christ died for our sins, rose from the dead to offer us eternal life, and stands ready now to forgive our sins. But each of us must choose for ourselves if we will follow our way or His. When Jesus was on earth He said, *"Enter ye in at the strait gate: for wide is the gate, and broad is the*

---

1   Isaiah 53:6
2   Romans 3:23
3   John 14:6

way, that leadeth to destruction, and many there be which go in threat: Because strait is the gate, and narrow is the way, which leadeth unto life, and few there be that find it."[4]

There are only two destinations: eternity in Heaven with God or separated from God forever in Hell. All roads cannot lead to the same place. Our way leads us *from* God; Christ's way leads us *to* God. If you continue on the path you are on now, where will you spend eternity? You must determine your destination.

✝ Discover the companionship of Christ.

The journey is always better with a companion, someone with whom we share both the joys and trials of the trip. This is why Jesus Christ came to this earth. He traveled this same road for thirty-three years. The Son of God is not a person far away who, *"cannot be touched with the feeling of our infirmities; but was in all points tempted like as we are, yet without sin."*[5] He knows where you are and what you are facing!

Even more, He wants to make the journey with you right now. This personal relationship begins at the moment that

---

4   Matthew 7:13-14
5   Hebrews 4:15

you place your faith in Him and call on Him to be your Savior. *"That if thou shalt confess with thy mouth the Lord Jesus, and shalt believe in thine heart that God hath raised him from the dead, thou shalt be saved."*[6]

When a person comes to know Christ, two things are made sure: they will live with Christ forever in Heaven, and Christ comes to live in their heart now! In one of the most famous psalms, Psalm 23, David explains it this way, *"Surely goodness and mercy shall follow me all the days of my life: and I will dwell in the house of the LORD for ever."*[7]

To follow Christ is to have Him make the journey with you, never alone! In some of His last words to the first disciples He said, *"...I am with you alway, even unto the end of the world. Amen."*[8] There will be difficulties along the way, but He will guard us and guide us at every step.

✝ Know what to do at important intersections.

Intersections are turning points. At each of them there is a decision to be made. Life is full of decisions, but the

---

6   Romans 10:9
7   Psalm 23:6
8   Matthew 28:20

most important ones are the ones that affect eternity. Today you are standing at one of those crossroads. You will either choose to follow Christ or to continue on your own way. Remember that a wrong turn doesn't lead to the right place! The right turn is to repent and believe on Christ.[9]

There are two paths and we all must decide which one we will take. Jesus said, *"He that believeth on him is not condemned: but he that believeth not is condemned already, because he hath not believed in the name of the only begotten Son of God."*[10] Will you believe on Christ today?

Call on Him now! "Dear God, be merciful to me a sinner. I know that you died for me and believe that you rose from the dead. Please forgive my sin and come into my life. I trust you now as my personal Savior. Thank you for giving me the free gift of eternal life. In Jesus' name, Amen."

This is the beginning of your journey with Jesus. He promises those who belong to Him, *"I will never leave thee, nor forsake thee."*[11] We would love to hear from you and help you as you begin to walk with Christ.

Visit us at **enjoyingthejourney.org** to take the next step.

---

9   Acts 20:21
10   John 3:18
11   Hebrews 13:5